D1444710

F/A-18E/F SUPER HORNETS

BY DENNY VON FINN

EPIC

BELLWETHER MEDIA · MINNEAPOLIS, MN

EPIC BOOKS are no ordinary books. They burst with intense action, high-speed heroics, and shadows of the unknown. Are you ready for an Epic adventure?

This edition first published in 2013 by Bellwether Media, Inc.

No part of this publication may be reproduced in whole or in part without written permission of the publisher. For information regarding permission, write to Bellwether Media, Inc., Attention: Permissions Department, 5357 Penn Avenue South, Minneapolis, MN 55419.

Library of Congress Cataloging-in-Publication Data

Von Finn, Denny.
 F/A-18E/F Super Hornets / by Denny Von Finn.
    p. cm. – (Epic books: military vehicles)
 Includes bibliographical references and index.
 Summary: "Engaging images accompany information about F/A-18E/F Super Hornets. The combination of high-interest subject matter and light text is intended for students in grades 2 through 7"–Provided by publisher.
 Audience: Grades 2-7.
 ISBN 978-1-60014-818-7 (hbk. : alk. paper)
 1. Hornet (Jet fighter plane)–Juvenile literature. I. Title.
 UG1242.F5V657 2013
 623.74'63–dc23   2012007877

Printed in the United States of America, North Mankato, MN.

TABLE OF CONTENTS

F/A-18E/F SUPER HORNETS

A Super Hornet prepares to take off from an **aircraft carrier**. It is armed and ready for a tough **mission**.

A sailor on **deck** waves the pilot ahead. The Super Hornet roars into the air to confront an enemy plane.

Super Hornet Fact

Super Hornets can take off from both aircraft carriers and land bases.

The Super Hornet's **radar** finds
the target. The **weapons systems officer**
fires a **missile**. An explosion fills the sky.
The mission is a success!

CREW, ENGINES, AND WEAPONS

A pilot flies alone in the F/A-18E Super Hornet. The F/A-18F also has a weapons systems officer.

WEAPONS SYSTEMS OFFICER

PILOT

VFA-11 S

LT HUDSPETH DINGLE

LT HESS ANOYA

270

ADAN SUTTON

Two jet engines power the Super Hornet to **supersonic** speeds. The Super Hornet is armed with missiles, bombs, and a 20mm gun.

SUPERSONIC SPEED

BOMBS

MISSILE

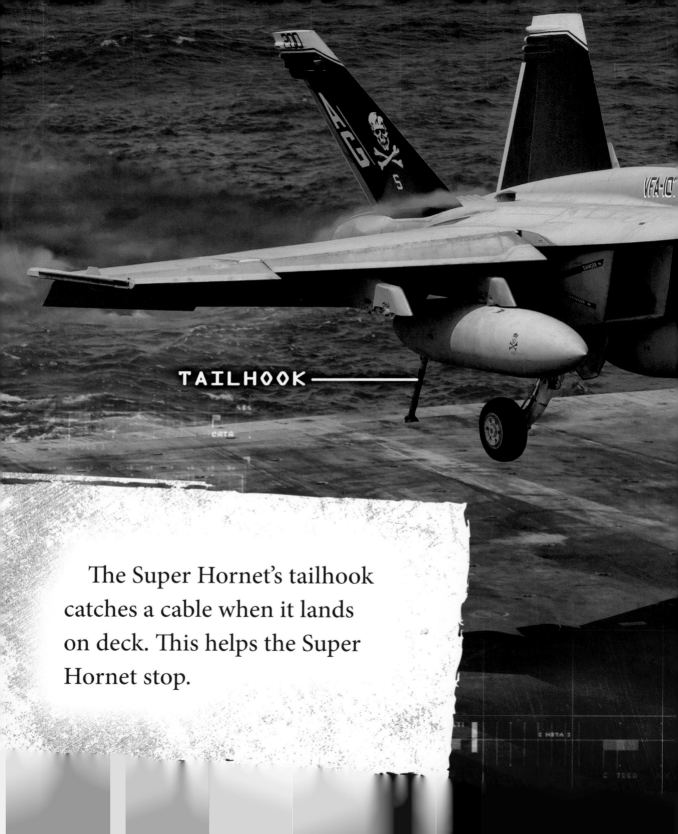

TAILHOOK ———————

The Super Hornet's tailhook catches a cable when it lands on deck. This helps the Super Hornet stop.

Super Hornet Fact

The Super Hornet's wings fold up. This saves space on an aircraft carrier.

15

SUPER HORNET
MISSIONS

121

VX-23

NAVY
NAVAIR

F/A-18F
166449

THREAT DET

Super Hornets fill many roles for the United States Navy. They serve as **strike fighters**. They learn about the enemy on **recon** missions.

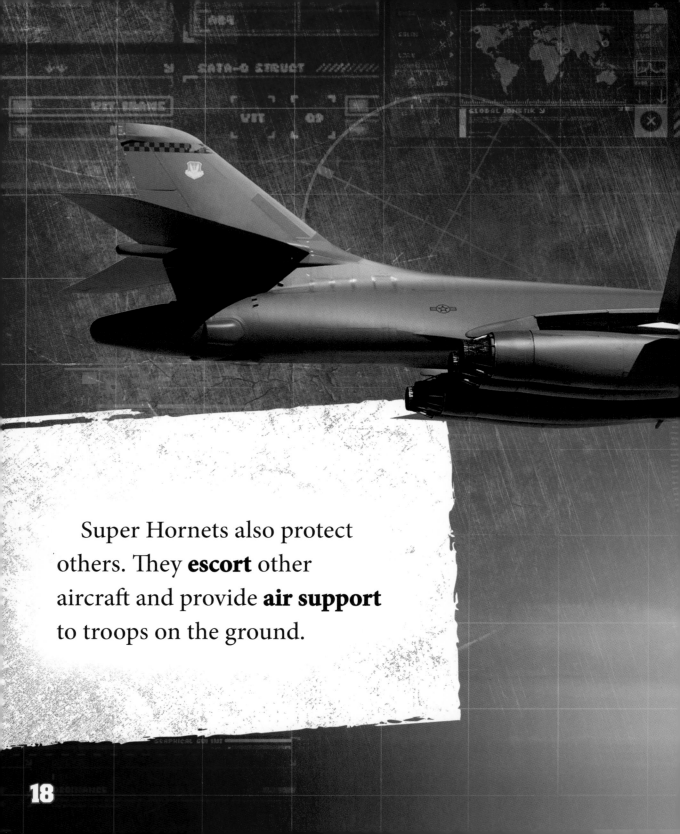

Super Hornets also protect others. They **escort** other aircraft and provide **air support** to troops on the ground.

The U.S. Navy owns more than 500 Super Hornets.

VEHICLE BREAKDOWN: F/A-18E/F SUPER HORNET

Used By:	U.S. Navy
Entered Service:	1999
Length:	60.3 feet (18.4 meters)
Height:	16 feet (4.9 meters)
Wingspan:	44.9 feet (13.7 meters)
Weight (Fully Loaded):	66,000 pounds (29,930 kilograms)
Top Speed:	1,380 miles (2,220 kilometers) per hour
Maximum Range:	1,458 miles (2,346 kilometers)
Ceiling:	50,000 feet (15,240 meters)
Crew:	1 or 2
Weapons:	20mm gun, missiles, bombs
Nickname:	Rhino
Primary Missions:	striking, escorting, recon, air support

Super Hornets have performed many missions in the **War on Terror**. These tough fighters go anywhere help is needed.

GLOSSARY

air support—a type of mission that involves flying close to and protecting troops on the ground

aircraft carrier—a large ship that jet fighters can take off from and land on

deck—the large, flat surface on top of an aircraft carrier; jet fighters take off from and land on the deck.

escort—to travel alongside and protect

missile—an explosive that is guided to a target

mission—a military task

radar—a system that uses radio waves to locate targets

recon—a type of mission that involves gathering information about the enemy

strike fighters—small, quick military aircraft used mostly to destroy targets on the ground

supersonic—faster than the speed of sound; sound travels about 760 miles (1,225 kilometers) per hour at sea level.

War on Terror—a conflict that began in 2001; the War on Terror has been fought in Afghanistan, Pakistan, and Iraq.

weapons systems officer—the crew member in an F/A-18F Super Hornet who is in charge of the fighter's weapons

TO LEARN MORE

At the Library

Bledsoe, Karen and Glen. *Fighter Planes: Fearless Fliers.* Berkeley Heights, N.J.: Enslow Publishers, 2006.

Trumbauer, Lisa. *Fighter Jet.* Chicago, Ill.: Raintree, 2008.

Von Finn, Denny. *Jet Fighters.* Minneapolis, Minn.: Bellwether Media, 2010.

On the Web

Learning more about Super Hornets is as easy as 1, 2, 3.

1. Go to www.factsurfer.com.

2. Enter "Super Hornets" into the search box.

3. Click the "Surf" button and you will see a list of related Web sites.

With factsurfer.com, finding more information is just a click away.

INDEX